MW01002582

The Story of John the Baptist
Accurately retold from the Bible
(from the books of Matthew, Mark, Luke
and John)
by Carine Mackenzie

Illustrations by
Duncan McLaren
Cover design by Daniel van Straaten

© Copyright 1985 Christian Focus Publications
ISBN 978-1-84550-164-8

New edition 1989
Reprinted 1992, 1998, 2000, 2006, 2009, 2012 and 2013

Published in Great Britain by
Christian Focus Publications
Geanies House, Fearn, Tain, Ross-shire, IV20 1TW, Scotland.
www.christianfocus.com

Printed in China

John was a very special messenger from God. Jesus said that there was no man greater than John the Baptist.

Before John was born, his mother Elizabeth and his father Zacharias lived in a town in the hilly countryside near to Jerusalem. They were old and still had no children and must often have wondered if their prayers for a child would ever be answered.

Elizabeth and Zacharias loved the Lord God and lived holy lives, obeying God's commandments. Zacharias was a priest in God's temple at Jerusalem.

When it was his turn he would take his place there to perform the various duties.

One day Zacharias was in the temple near to the altar, while the people were outside praying. Suddenly an angel appeared standing on the right hand side of the altar. When Zacharias saw him, he was very afraid.

The angel said, 'Do not be frightened, Zacharias. Your prayer has been heard. Your wife Elizabeth shall have a baby son and you shall call him, John.'

The angel told Zacharias more good news about his child. He would bring joy not only to Zacharias and Elizabeth but also to many others. Many people would be turned from their sins to love the Lord Jesus through John's preaching.

Zacharias could hardly believe his ears.

'I am an old man and my wife is old too,' he said.

The angel replied, 'My name is Gabriel and God has sent me to tell you this good news. Because you do not believe me, you will be struck dumb and you will not be able to speak until my words have come true!'

Zacharias was punished for disbelieving.
Do you believe God's word when you
hear it or read it?
You too deserve to be punished if you do
not believe what God tells
you in the Bible.

The people outside began to
wonder why Zacharias was taking such a
long time in the temple. He came out at
last but could not
speak to them.

He could only make signs.
After Zacharias had finished his
time of duty in the temple,
he went back to his own home.

Before long Elizabeth was expecting a baby. She was very pleased and knew that God had been kind to her.

Six months later Elizabeth had a visit from her cousin Mary. Mary had just received wonderful news from the angel Gabriel that she would be the mother of Jesus, the Son of God. As soon as Mary came into Elizabeth's house she called out a greeting to her.

Elizabeth felt the baby moving inside her for joy. Elizabeth's baby was a special child and even before he was born, God the Holy Spirit had made him respond to the Lord Jesus Christ.

Elizabeth was very happy when her baby boy was born. Her neighbours and cousins heard how good the Lord had been to her. They were delighted too.

When the baby was eight days old he was to be named and some friends thought that he would be called Zacharias after his father. His mother said, 'Oh no, he shall be called John.' 'None of your relations are called John,' they objected. They then made signs to Zacharias to see what name he wanted. Zacharias asked for something to write on, and he wrote, 'His name is John!'

Immediately Zacharias was able to speak again. The first words he spoke were words of praise to God.

Zacharias told the people that the baby John would be a preacher one day. He would warn people about sin and point the people to the Lord Jesus. How could Zacharias know about this? He had been told by God, the Holy Spirit.

John grew up strong and healthy, living in the quiet desert land of Judea. He lived a simple life. His clothes were made of camel's hair and he wore a belt of animal skin. His food was locusts and wild honey. His work was very important. He was a preacher.

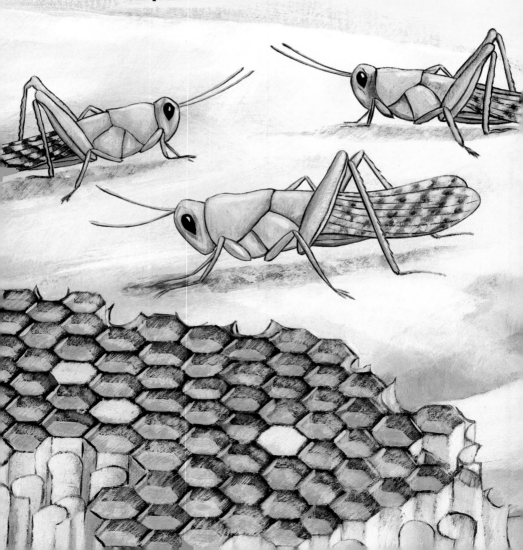

'Turn from your sins,' he told the crowds. 'Believe the gospel. The Kingdom of God is near.'

The message John gave is a good message for you. You too must turn from your sin and believe the good news of the gospel. The good news is that Jesus, God's Son came into the world so that whoever believes in him will have everlasting life with him in heaven.

Trust in Jesus now. Do not put it off till a later date. Tomorrow may be too late.

Many people from Judea and Jerusalem were baptised by John in the River Jordan. They confessed their sins and were sorry for them and were made willing to turn from their sins to God. Being baptised in the water was an outward symbol of having their sins washed away.

When the church leaders from Jerusalem heard about John preaching, they sent priests out to question him. 'Who are you?' they asked. 'I am not Christ,' he answered. 'Are you a prophet?' they asked again. 'I am just a voice crying in the wilderness. The man coming after me is much more important that I am. In fact I do not even feel worthy to bend down and unfasten his shoes.'

John was speaking about Jesus.

The next day John saw Jesus coming towards him and he said, 'Behold the Lamb of God who takes away the sin of the world.'

Jesus died on the cross so that the sins of his people could be taken away. If you have faith in Jesus, your sins are forgiven and washed completely away. Ask the Lord Jesus to give you this faith.

One day Jesus came to the river Jordan to see John. He asked John to baptise him. John was surprised. 'I need to be baptised by you and yet you are coming to me?' he said. Jesus persuaded him that this was the right thing to do. Jesus had no sin, so his baptism did not mean having his sins washed away. He was baptised as an example to others and to show us that although he was God, he was also fully man.

When Jesus came up out of the water of the River Jordan, the heavens opened up and the Spirit of God came down upon him, shaped like a dove. A voice was heard from heaven saying, 'This is my beloved Son in whom I am well pleased.' God was pleased with what Jesus had done.

John always gave the most important place to Jesus. His preaching was pointing to him. His job was to prepare the way for Jesus. 'I must become less important' he said, 'and Jesus must become greater.'

John preached against the sins of the people. King Herod was a sinful man and John told him about his sin. Herod had married his brother's wife, Herodias. John told him that this was against God's law. Herod was not sorry for his sin. He and Herodias were very angry with John.

Herod locked John up in prison.
He would really have liked to kill John
but he was afraid to do that because the
people believed that John was a prophet.

In prison John heard about the wonderful work that Jesus was doing in the country. He sent two of his friends to Jesus with a message.

'Are you the one that is come from God, or should we look for another man?

Jesus sent back a reply. 'Tell John about what you have seen and heard. The blind can see, the lame can walk, the lepers are cleansed and the deaf hear, the dead are raised to life and the poor have the gospel preached to them.'

This reassured John that Jesus was indeed the Son of God.

On his birthday, Herod had a big party. He invited all the important men in the land. Herodias' daughter danced for Herod.

He and his guests were so pleased with her that Herod said, 'I will give you anything you ask for, even half of my kingdom.'

What a fantastic offer! What would she ask for? Would it be jewels perhaps, fine horses, a palace?

No. After speaking with her mother, the girl came back to Herod. 'Give me John the Baptist's head on a big plate!'

King Herod was very upset when he heard this request but he did not want to back down on his promise. He did not want to look weak in front of his friends.

He sent the dreadful command to
the prison to have John beheaded.
The head was brought into the
palace on a large plate and
given to the young dancer.
She brought it to her mother.
John's friends took his body
from the prison and buried it.
Then they went to find Jesus
to tell him all that had happend.

When you are sad or have a problem,
big or little, the best thing to do is to
tell Jesus. He is the very best friend
you can have. You can tell him
everything in prayer.

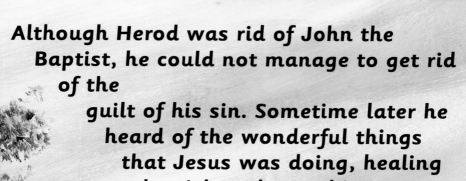

Although Herod was rid of John the Baptist, he could not manage to get rid of the guilt of his sin. Sometime later he heard of the wonderful things that Jesus was doing, healing the sick and preaching. Herod was afraid that this was John raised from the dead. It brought back guilty memories to him.

If you trust in Jesus, he has promised that your sins are forgiven. The guilt is washed away, because Jesus has taken the punishment himself when he died on the cross. God has promised to remember these sins no more.

All his life John loved the Lord. His great work was to warn the people about their sin and to tell them of the Lord Jesus, the Saviour. Will you follow his advice to look to Jesus, the Lamb of God who takes away the sin of the world?